2/20/07    EPI    22.60

## DATE DUE

| NOV 1 7 2016 | | |
|---|---|---|
| | | |
| | | |
| | | |
| | | |
| | | |
| | | |
| | | |
| | | |
| | | |
| | | |
| | | |

Demco

*Multicultural Crafts Kids Can Do!*

# Middle Eastern Crafts Kids Can Do!

*Sarah Hartman*

**Enslow Elementary**
an imprint of

**Enslow Publishers, Inc.**

| | |
|---|---|
| 40 Industrial Road | PO Box 38 |
| Box 398 | Aldershot |
| Berkeley Heights, NJ 07922 | Hants GU12 6BP |
| USA | UK |

http://www.enslow.com

Enslow Elementary, an imprint of Enslow Publishers, Inc.

Enslow Elementary® is a registered trademark of Enslow Publishers, Inc.

**Library of Congress Cataloging-in-Publication Data**

Hartman, Sarah.
   Middle Eastern crafts kids can do! / Sarah Hartman.
      p. cm. — (Multicultural crafts kids can do!)
   Includes bibliographical references and index.
   ISBN 0-7660-2456-3
   1. Handicraft—Middle East—Juvenile literature. I. Title. II. Series.
   TT113.5H37 2006
   745.50956—dc22
                         2005028115

Printed in the United States of America

10 9 8 7 6 5 4 3 2 1

**To Our Readers:** We have done our best to make sure all Internet Addresses in this book were active and appropriate when we went to press. However, the author and the publisher have no control over and assume no liability for the material available on those Internet sites or on other Web sites they may link to. Any comments or suggestions can be sent by e-mail to comments@enslow.com or to the address on the back cover.

Every effort has been made to locate all copyright holders of material used in this book. If any errors or omissions have occurred, corrections will be made in future editions of this book.

**Illustration Credits:** Crafts prepared by June Ponte; photography by Lindsay Pries. © 1996–2004 ArtToday, Inc., p. 10; © 1999 Artville, LLC., p. 5; Corel Corporation, pp. 4, 6, 12; © 2005 JupiterImages, pp. 13 (glass jar), 18; Saudi Aramco World/PADIA, pp. 14, 22.

**Cover Illustration:** Photography by Lindsay Pries.

# Contents

Safety Note: Be sure to ask for help from an adult, if needed, to complete these crafts!

# Introduction

The crafts of the Middle East date back thousands of years, before the time of pharaohs and mummies. The crafters of countries like Egypt, Syria, Iran, and Israel have been weaving, sculpting, and painting for many years.

The crafts of the Middle East are not only old. They are also varied. Crafts range from nomad tent decorations to items found in pyramids.

Crafts come from mythologies and ancient traditions, such as Egyptian hieroglyphics and the ancient art of wood inlay practiced in Syria.

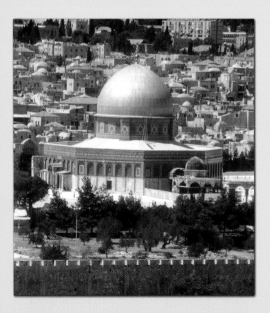

Crafts also come from religious beliefs and practices. Prayer rugs are an Islamic craft, while dreidels are a Jewish toy for Hanukkah.

By combining a few craft supplies with your imagination, you can make Middle Eastern crafts. Take part in the rich history of these nations by learning about their culture and crafts.

*This is Dome of the Rock in Jerusalem, Israel.*

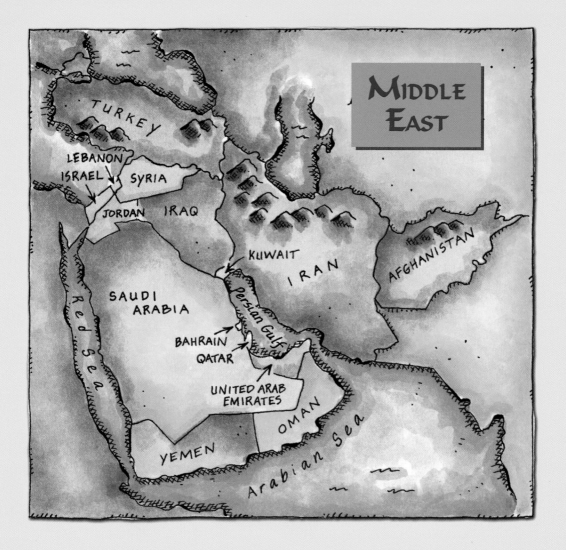

MIDDLE EAST

TURKEY

LEBANON
ISRAEL
SYRIA
JORDAN
IRAQ
KUWAIT
IRAN
AFGHANISTAN

SAUDI ARABIA

Red Sea

Persian Gulf

BAHRAIN
QATAR
UNITED ARAB EMIRATES

OMAN

YEMEN

Arabian Sea

# Hieroglyphic Wrapping Paper and Bags

*Egyptian writings, or hieroglyphics, are over three thousand years old. The oldest hieroglyphics are just pictures that tell stories. The ancient Egyptians created an alphabet of twenty-four letters from hieroglyphics. Hieroglyphics were used to record histories, decorate doors and walls, and cover tombs.*

## What You Will Need:

- brown packing paper
- brown paper bags
- new kitchen sponges
- poster paint
- markers
- scissors

1. Trace the hieroglyphic patterns onto clean, unused sponges. Trace only the thick black lines. Cut them out. (See page 27 for the pattern.)

2. Dip the sponges in paint and press them to brown packing paper. Make rows of different hieroglyphics for wrapping paper.

3. For bags, stamp rows of hieroglyphics or stamp one in the center of the bag.

4. Add the details of the hieroglyphics, like eyes, with a marker.

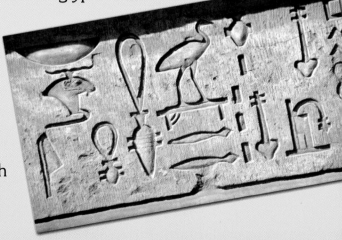

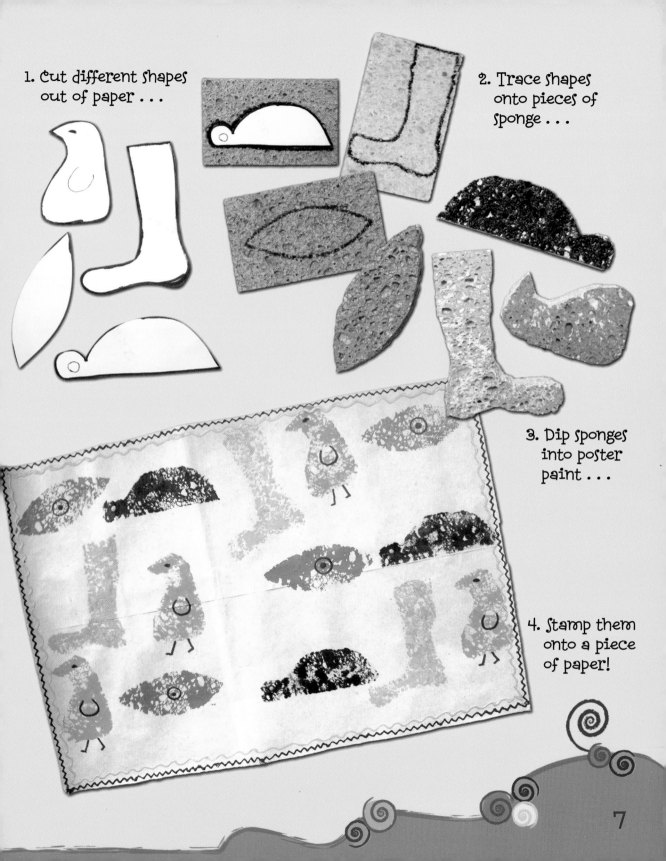

1. Cut different shapes out of paper . . .

2. Trace shapes onto pieces of sponge . . .

3. Dip sponges into poster paint . . .

4. Stamp them onto a piece of paper!

# Turkish Evil Eye Luck Charm

*The Turkish Evil Eye is a popular charm against bad luck or evil spirits. The charm can be worn as jewelry or hung as decoration.*

## What You Will Need:

- large wooden bead
- key-chain ring
- thick yarn
- white and blue poster paint
- paintbrush

1. Paint the bead blue and let dry.

2. Paint a white eye with blue center on the bead. Let dry.

3. Cut a length of yarn. Pass the yarn through the key chain.

4. String the bead onto both ends of yarn. Hold both ends of yarn together and tie knots until the bead cannot pass over the knot.

5. Put keys on the key ring to use charm as a key chain. Or attach the key ring to a zipper on a backpack to use as a zipper pull.

1. Paint a wooden bead blue and then paint the eye . . .

2. String some yarn through a key chain . . .

3. Add your painted bead and knot in place!

9

# Poster Board Prayer Rug Collage

*Each day, a Muslim must pray five times. Muslims do not have to pray in a mosque, but must pray on a clean surface. A clean surface is one that has not been made dirty by shoes or dirty feet. When a Muslim lays a prayer rug down, he creates a clean surface on which to pray. A prayer rug also has a mihrab on it, like the mihrab on a mosque wall. The mihrab indicates the direction of Mecca and prayer.*

## What You Will Need:

- poster board
- construction paper
- scissors
- glue

1. Cut out strips of different colored paper.
2. Create your own pattern and glue the paper to the poster board. Let dry.
3. When glue is dry, the poster can be laid on the floor like a prayer rug.

*This is the Prophet's Mosque in Medina, Saudi Arabia.*

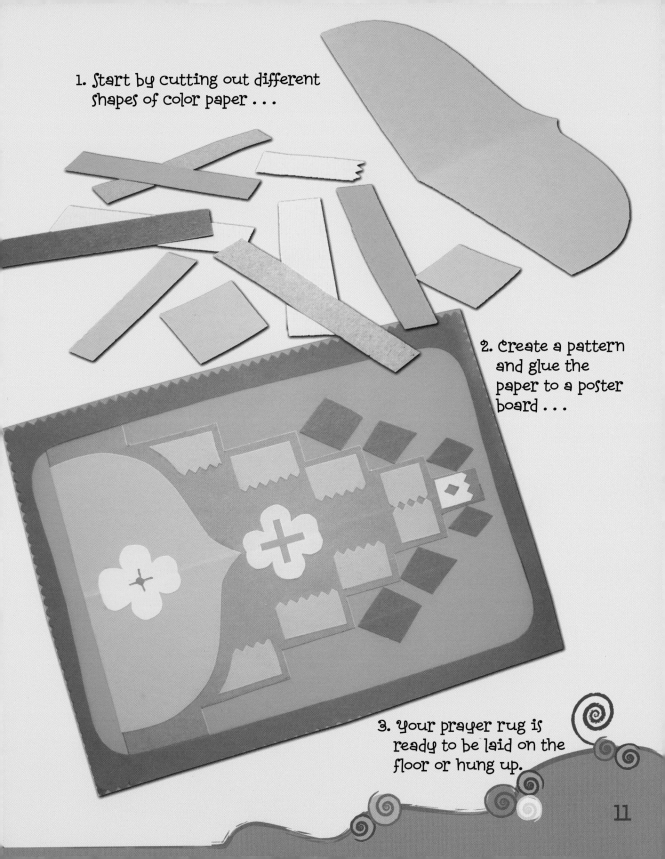

1. Start by cutting out different shapes of color paper . . .

2. Create a pattern and glue the paper to a poster board . . .

3. Your prayer rug is ready to be laid on the floor or hung up.

# Pitharia

*Pitharia are large clay jars that were made in Cyprus. They were used in preparing wine. Pitharia were also used to store things in. At one time, an entire village in Cyprus made these clay jars. The jars were hard to move because they were so large. Sometimes, a crafter traveled to someone's house to make the jar there. That way, the jar would not have to be moved. Make a small version of these giant jars.*

## What You Will Need:

- baby food jar, washed and dried
- white modeling clay
- toothpicks
- red poster paint
- paintbrush

1. Form clay around a clean baby food jar. If you wish, make handles. Use toothpicks to make grooves in the clay around the jar. Make grooves wavy or straight. Make many grooves or only a few.

2. Let clay stand around baby food jar overnight, or until hard.

3. Brush red paint lightly onto clay. Make some areas darker, some areas lighter, and leave streaks.

4. Let dry, then use the jar for holding things.

*These are ancient ruins in Cyprus.*

1. Form modeling clay
   around a small food jar . . .

2. Let dry until
   hard and then
   paint it!

# foam Inlay Wall Hanging

*Intarsia is an ancient craft of laying pieces of wood together to form a picture. Wood is inlaid to decorate furniture, boxes, or make pictures for walls. The art form is very detailed and hard to learn. Intarsia is still practiced in Syria and Egypt.*

## What You Will Need:

- craft foam sheets
- scissors
- glue
- pencil
- yarn or ribbon
- poster board

1. Trace the Inlay Wall Hanging pattern on two pieces of different colored craft foam. (See page 27 for the pattern.)

2. Cut out on all the black lines.

3. Fit the pieces of different colors together, like two puzzles.

4. Glue the foam pieces to a piece of poster board. Let dry.

5. Glue a piece of ribbon or yarn to the back of poster board in a loop. Let dry.

6. Use the loop to hang on the wall.

1. Trace pattern onto craft foam . . .

2. Fit the pieces together like a puzzle . . .

3. Glue onto poster board and add a bright ribbon!

# Perfume and Oil Bottles

*Throughout history, the Middle East has been known for its oils and perfumes. At one time, rich men and women from Europe paid high prices for oils from the East. They used the oils to cover bad smells. Design a perfume bottle and fill it with modern bath oil to make a unique gift.*

## What You Will Need:

- plastic water bottle with paper completely removed
- poster paint or paint markers
- plastic rhinestones or sequins
- glue
- paintbrush
- black puff paint
- ribbon (optional)

1. Cover the plastic bottle with black puff paint lines. Let dry.

2. Use paint or paint markers to color the spaces between the black lines. Only use one coat of paint. Let dry.

3. Glue plastic rhinestones or sequins around the bottle or to the bottle cap.

4. Fill bottle with colored water for decoration, or scented bath oil to give as a gift.

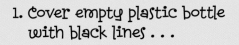

1. Cover empty plastic bottle with black lines . . .

2. Use paint to color the spaces in between . . .

3. Finish off with a fancy ribbon and rhinestones!

17

# Dreidel

*The dreidel game is played during Hanukkah. The dreidel is a top with four sides. On each side is a Hebrew letter. The four letters stand for "Nes Gadol Hayah Shom," which means "A great miracle happened there."*

## What You Will Need:

- poster board
- black marker
- scissors
- glue
- plastic bottle cap

1. Trace the dreidel pattern on the poster board. (See page 28 for the pattern.) Include the four letters. Looking at the dreidel pattern, from left to right, the letters are Shin, Hei, Gimel, and Nun. Cut out the traced pattern on solid black lines.

2. Fold all pieces in on dotted lines.

3. Glue the dreidel together by putting glue on the tabs and pressing against joining pieces. Glue a plastic bottle cap to the top of the dreidel.

4. Let all glue dry before playing the dreidel game (game rules can be found on page 29).

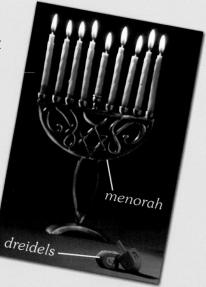

menorah

dreidels

1. Cut out dreidel pattern . . .

2. Fold and glue the cut-out . . .

3. Decorate with bright colors and glue on a plastic bottle top!

19

# Ships of Oman Notecard

*In ancient times, Omani ships traveled from Asia to Africa. The wooden sailing ships brought goods throughout the known world. In the 1600s, Omani ships controlled most of the trade on the East African coast. Make one of these famous sailing ships as a notecard. Write a message inside and give it to a friend.*

## What You Will Need:

- brown and light-colored construction paper
- white construction paper, 8 ½ x 11
- pencil
- crayons or markers
- scissors
- glue

1. Trace section 1 of the ship onto brown construction paper and cut out. (See page 28 for the pattern.)

2. Trace section 2 and 3 of the ship onto light-colored construction paper and cut out. (See page 28 for the pattern.)

3. Glue sections 2 and 3 to section 1 to make sails. The sails may overlap. Let dry. If you wish, decorate the sails using markers and crayons.

4. Fold a piece of white construction paper in half to make a card. Glue the ship to the front of the card. Let dry.

5. Write a letter inside and send it to a friend. Or make several notecards and give them as a gift.

1. Cut out ship and sails from the patterns . . .

2. Decorate with markers and glitter . . .

3. Glue to a piece of paper folded in half!

# Bedouin Tent Decoration

*Bedouins are nomads who live in the deserts of the Middle East and North Africa. They travel in tribes across the desert, living in tents. Sometimes they decorate their tents with woven rugs and hangings.*

## What You Will Need:

- construction paper
- glue
- scissors
- pipe cleaners
- beads
- ruler
- pencil

1. Use a ruler to copy the Bedouin Tent Decoration pattern onto construction paper. Make it as big or small as you wish. (See page 26 for the pattern.)

2. Cut on all the lines drawn across construction paper.

3. Cut strips of construction paper out of a different color. Weave strips into paper with lines cut out. Glue down the ends.

4. Punch two holes in the top of weaved paper. Attach a pipe cleaner to the holes to make a hanger for the decoration.

5. Punch holes along the bottom of the weaved paper. Hang pipe cleaners from the holes. Coil pipe cleaners into patterns, or attach beads to pipe cleaners.

6. Hang the decoration up on a wall or in doorway.

1. Use a ruler to help you draw the pattern . . .

2. Cut strips of different color paper and weave them with the pattern . . .

3. Add beads and pipe cleaners, and your decoration is ready to hang up!

# Ramadan Hanging Ornaments

*Ramadan is a holy month for Muslims. It falls during the ninth month of the Islamic calendar. During Ramadan, people pray, fast, and do works of charity for those in need. Since Ramadan begins and ends with a new moon, the moon and stars are sometimes used as Ramadan decorations.*

## What You Will Need:

- poster board
- glitter
- markers
- glue
- yarn
- hole punch
- scissors

1. Draw a crescent moon shape on a piece of poster board. (See page 26 for the pattern.) Cut it out and use it to trace thirty moons on the poster board. Cut out all the shapes.

2. Decorate the moons with glitter or markers.

3. Punch a hole in the top of each moon and tie yarn through.

4. Hang the ornaments along a wall or door frame.

5. For each day of Ramadan, remove one ornament.

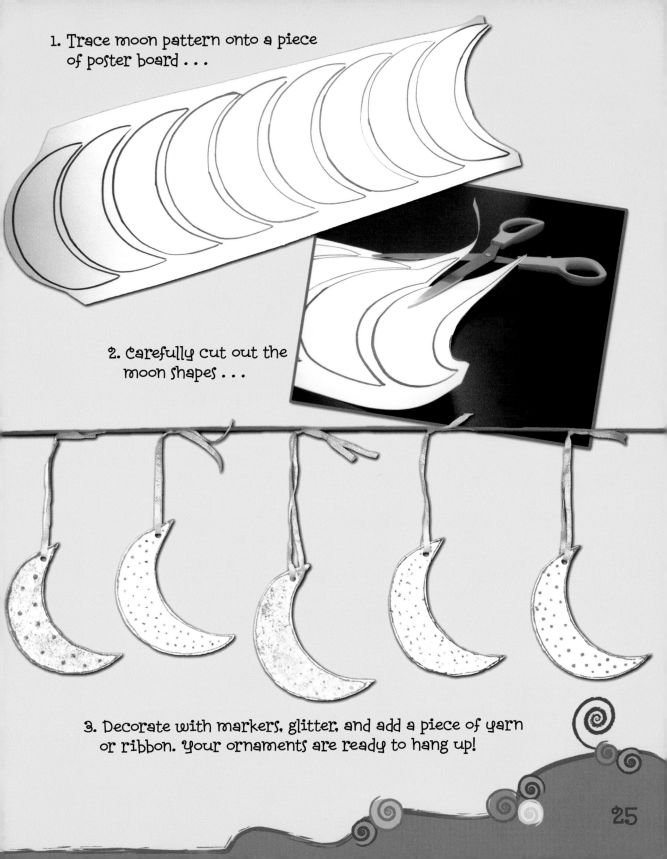

1. Trace moon pattern onto a piece of poster board . . .

2. Carefully cut out the moon shapes . . .

3. Decorate with markers, glitter, and add a piece of yarn or ribbon. Your ornaments are ready to hang up!

#  Patterns

Use a copier to enlarge or shrink the design to the size you want.

*Use tracing paper to copy the patterns on these pages. Ask an adult to help you cut and trace the shapes onto construction paper.*

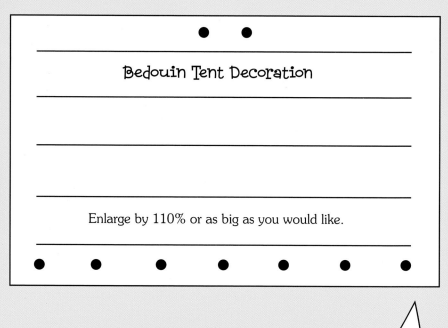

Bedouin Tent Decoration

Enlarge by 110% or as big as you would like.

Ramadan Hanging Ornament

At 100%

foam Inlay
Wall Hanging

Enlarge by 160%

Hieroglyphic
Wrapping Paper
and Bags

Enlarge by 145%

27

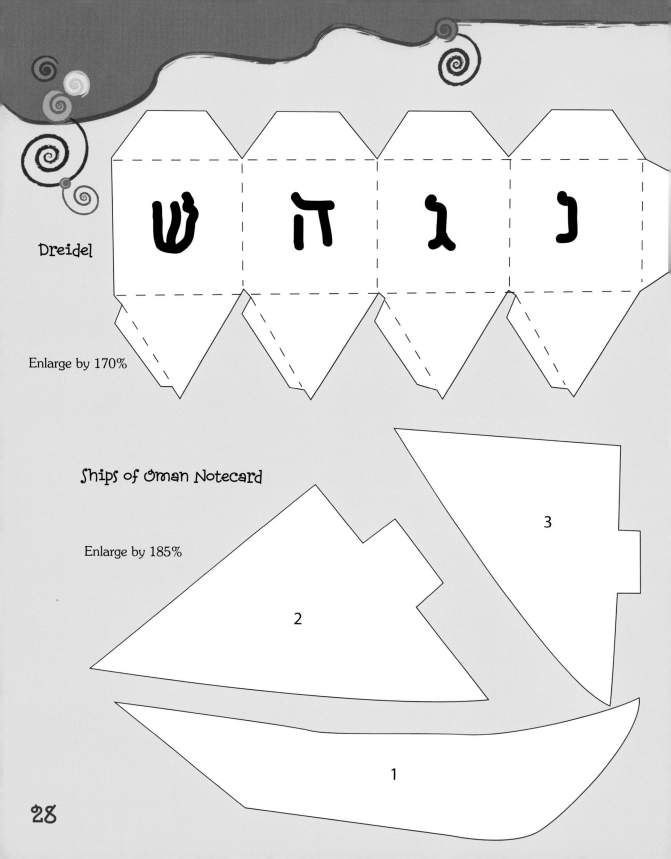

Dreidel

Enlarge by 170%

Ships of Oman Notecard

Enlarge by 185%

# Game Rules

## Dreidel

1. Each player starts with ten pieces of candy.

2. Each player puts a piece of candy into the middle.

3. Each player spins the dreidel.

4. If the dreidel stops on Nun, the player wins nothing.

5. If the dreidel stops on Gimel, the player takes all of the candy in the middle.

6. If the dreidel stops on Hei, the player takes half of the candy in the middle.

7. If the dreidel stops on Shin, the player puts a piece of candy in the middle.

# Reading About

## Books

Cheshire, Gerard, and Paula Hammond. *The Middle East*. Broomall, Penn.: Mason Crest Publishers, 2003.

Ganeri, Anita. *Muslim Festivals Throughout the Year*. Mankato, Minn.: Smart Apple Media, 2003.

Gibbons, Gail. *Mummies, Pyramids, and Pharaohs: A Book About Ancient Egypt*. New York: Little, Brown, 2004.

Gnojewski, Carol. *Ramadan—A Muslim Time of Fasting, Prayer, and Celebration*. Berkeley Heights, N.J.: Enslow Publishers, Inc., 2004.

Khan, Aisha Karen. *What You Will See Inside a Mosque*. Woodstock, Vt.: Skylight Paths Pub., 2003.

Podwal, Mark. *A Sweet Year: A Taste of the Jewish Holidays*. New York: Random House Children's Books, 2003.

## Internet Addresses

### Global Connections: The Middle East

<http://www.pbs.org/wgbh/globalconnections/
mideast/index.html>

*Learn more about the Middle East at this site.*

### Hieroglyphics

<http://www.kingtut-treasures.com/hiero.htm>

*Find out what your name would look like in hieroglyphics.*

# Index